LOOK AT ME NOW

LOOK AT ME NOW

Karen Hale

Editor: Don Gladden

XULON ELITE

Xulon Press Elite
2301 Lucien Way #415
Maitland, FL 32751
407.339.4217
www.xulonpress.com

© 2022 by Karen Hale

Editor: Don Gladden

All rights reserved solely by the author. The author guarantees all contents are original and do not infringe upon the legal rights of any other person or work. No part of this book may be reproduced in any form without the permission of the author. The views expressed in this book are not necessarily those of the publisher.

Due to the changing nature of the Internet, if there are any web addresses, links, or URLs included in this manuscript, these may have been altered and may no longer be accessible. The views and opinions shared in this book belong solely to the author and do not necessarily reflect those of the publisher. The publisher, therefore, disclaims responsibility for the views or opinions expressed within the work.

Unless otherwise indicated, Scripture quotations taken from the English Standard Version (ESV). Copyright © 2001 by Crossway, a publishing ministry of Good News Publishers. Used by permission. All rights reserved.

Paperback ISBN-13: 978-1-66284-993-0
Ebook ISBN-13: 978-1-66284-994-7

Dedicated to all men, women, boys, and girls who have ever found themselves in a real life situation; causing you to say: "Look at me now."

THANKS to my Mom and Dad who taught me that, "Can't couldn't do anything." And to those who read this and encouraged me to move forward: Pastor Rick McNeely, Brian Easton, Susan Morris, and Brenda Morse who also took the time to edit. You are the kind of people who make the world go around. And a special thanks to Don Gladden for his many hours devoted to helping me get it right. If it were not for you, I am certain I would have to spend too much time wondering if this story would ever get told. Thanks again for making the pages speak clearly.

Table of Contents

Chapter 1: A Good Name is Chosen 1

Chapter 2: God is Watching Over You 7

Chapter 3: Double Trouble 13

Chapter 4: Never Ending Trial 21

Chapter 5: Life Behind the Walls 27

Chapter 6: From Boy to Man 33

Chapter 7: Changes were Made 39

Chapter 8: Keeping Up the Pace 43

Chapter 9: The Ups and Downs 49

Poems by Dustin C. Clover 53

Foreword

Travel with Karen as she takes you down the path of a family that refused to give up, and a young man that finally did.

Look At Me Now is a journey of discovery, recovery, and redemption.

This true story of hope that can only be found in God, and a reminder that no matter how far you stray or how lost you feel, Jesus is still your guiding light home.

Pastor Rick McNeely

Preface
20/20 - A TRUE-LIFE STORY

HAVE YOU EVER heard the expression, "Hindsight is 20/20?" The meaning of this expression states: those choices that seemed difficult in the past now seem clear after the person knows what happened because of these choices. Understanding the scope of their past decisions and how it has affected the future can make one wish they could change their past.

Here is an example of, "Hindsight is 20/20." There were two boys, the first decided to cheat on a test. That boy could not understand how he got caught and told the second boy about it. The second boy was quick to tell him that he had told him not to cheat in the first place. The first boy replies with "well duh." Hindsight is 20/20. The first boy could clearly see his huge mistake and now knew the consequence of it. It not only cost him getting a failing grade for the test, but also caused him to fail the class. It never pays to not think things through before acting.

God should be our first "go to" for advice, especially when the knowledge of a wrong decision has some hard consequences.

> Proverbs 3:5-6 (ESV) "Trust in the Lord with all your heart and do not lean on your own understanding. In ALL your ways acknowledge Him, and He will make your path straight."

> Psalm 32:8 (ESV) "I will instruct you and teach you in the way you should go; I will counsel you with my eye upon you."

I believe that Psalm 32:8, if memorized, could and would stop a person and make them think. God says He will instruct us, teach us, and counsel us with His eye upon us; reminding us that He is watching our every move. This knowledge of His word would keep us from making a wrong decision.

The Bible also has scriptures on helping us make better decisions for our children.

> Proverbs 22:6 (ESV) "Train up a child in the way they should go and when they are old, they will not depart from it."

This is a hope that Christian parents have because we as parents are not assured that our children will stay on the right path. When a child starts making their own decisions, decisions that teach, some of the time because of that decision, they have to go through some things we rather they not have to experience. Hopefully they learn, but there are times we find ourselves looking up, because

Preface 20/20 - A TRUE-LIFE STORY

we have hit the bottom. When you are on the bottom there is no way to look except up. And God is waiting.

> Proverbs 29:15 (ESV) "The rod and reproof give wisdom, but a child left to himself brings shame to his mother."

Correcting our children shows them that we love them. Leaving children to themselves is obviously not good when it brings shame to their mother. Children are not mature enough to make wise decisions and will often get themselves into big trouble if left alone. We can talk until we are blue in the face instructing our children, they may or may not listen. We might tell them be good, stay in the house, and do not let anyone in. Thinking we have instructed enough to be able to leave them for a couple of hours, we leave. But, like the boy who decided to cheat on the test, those kids will always think if they do leave the house or have a friend over, they will survive the consequences.

God's Word is the best place to go when we need instruction on how to rear children. Two things are necessary. First, we must read that Word. And second, put that Word into practice. It is unfortunate for us to listen to the voices in our heads that cause us to make wrong decisions, like leaving our children to themselves.

Parents have to work in spite of summer vacation or snow days for the children. What is a parent to do? Years ago, women did not work outside the home. Mom was always home when the kids got home from school. Those times are long gone. So, children are left to themselves.

During WWII women had to go to work to help support their families and that didn't change after the war. When the men came home from the war, it took both the husband and the wife to provide for the family. That meant children were alone much of the time.

What happens when parents are not home? Children, even with chores to do, will gravitate to doing what they want, willing to pay the consequences to have what they want, fun. Then finding out later that being disobedient never turns out well.

This is the very thing that took place in homes across America and my sister and her husband were no exception to this fact. First, because of work, then needing to have a social agenda, they left their oldest daughter Jana in charge of Kristin and Dustin. They lived in the housing projects in our small community. Life in the housing projects helped to provide a leg up for families that needed assistance. But as years passed what was supposed to be a help ended up being a way of life for most that lived there. Change was inevitable but those changes were not all good.

Dustin was nine years old when the housing projects became known as The Hood. Even though he had a good family who tried to keep him from getting involved with the kids that lived in The Hood, Dustin started running the streets. It was not difficult to entice this little guy to walk his own walk. Staying with two older sisters was not fun, so he went looking for fun.

By the time he was sixteen, he was aware of street life and gang activity.

Preface 20/20 - A TRUE-LIFE STORY

It was 3 AM, my phone rang, and startled I answered the call. It was my sister Jan asking for prayer. Dustin and one other boy had gotten themselves in a mess of trouble. The police were in pursuit of two boys in a truck headed toward Herrin, Illinois, approximately twenty miles from Murphysboro. Jan had heard this over a police scanner. She also heard them say that one of the boys looked like Dustin Clover. It was a drug deal that had gone bad, with the involvement of guns. The young man who pulled a gun ended up being the victim. Heartbroken but trusting in an all-knowing God we prayed. The fact is, I prayed the rest of that morning. My prayer list consisted of Jan, Dustin, and all that was involved, especially the young man that went to the St. Louis hospital. I was not sure how my sister could handle much more of this kind of heart break. I found out later the young man with the gunshot wound had survived the night and was going to be okay. My nephew was in county jail.

Things do not happen quickly with our judicial system, so for months I prayed for and visited my nephew. Dustin was almost seventeen, just a baby in my eyes but not to a teenager who in his eyes knew everything. It was during all my praying that I felt God instructing me to draft this book. I was excited, yet I felt like He surely could find someone better than me.

I remembered the story of Moses when God told him he would lead God's people out of Egypt. Moses had excuses to not be the one, but God does not make mistakes. He calls the ones not equipped to do his bidding, because He will equip the one He calls and provide what it takes to finish what He starts. God had to really work on me to get me to understand this. I did not feel adequate, the only writing I had done was in high school English class. To this day I'm still not sure how I even got a B on a short story. I think the teacher liked me. I know God loves me and would help me through this writing project. Psalm 46:10 (ESV) "Be still and know that I am God." It was not about me; it is all about Him. Still yet, I did not have a clue where to begin.

I did attempt to draft the story. It fell apart. Why? Because I tried to do it on my own. I tried hard to do this in my own power; it was not right because I was not asking God and more importantly not listening to His voice. Before I realized what was happening, I had shed an ocean of tears. I knew I had heard God and I felt like He had deserted me, when it was me that left. I kept reminding myself of this. He tells us in His word that He will never leave us or forsake us. Hebrews 13:5 (ESV) "Never will I leave you or forsake you."

My nephew was in County jail when he penned this poem titled "Look at Me Now." He had not gone before the Judge for the crime and his conduct at this point.

So, I am starting at the beginning.

LOOK AT ME NOW

Look at me now, my life behind bars,
I can't see the world, not even the stars.
Just one more chance, I'll promise to do,
my heavenly father, I'll follow behind you.
He locked me up here, and allowed me to see,
what I could have been, when I was free!

Preface 20/20 - A TRUE-LIFE STORY

I took life for granted and misused my rights
I put up a shield to keep out the light.
Afraid of what others might have to say,
I remained in that life and decided to play.
The games that are out there, were not worth the trouble,
I'm trapped in the tank, with my life full of rubble.
I wish I had taken time to know Him before
then maybe I'd be on the other side of those doors.
Now, Christ Jesus I ask unto you,
break down these walls and let me walk through.

By Dustin Clover

    I felt this would be the title of the book I was to write, and Dustin and I agreed on the title... "LOOK AT ME NOW." After my first attempt, I was discouraged and gave up, even though I knew it was not over. I felt God tugging at me again to finish what needed to be completed. It could not have been written years ago because of all that has happened in the intervening years. I didn't have all the information that was needed.

Introduction

HAVE YOU EVER heard a child say, "I'm bored?" A nine-year-old looking for action may very well go find it. This is exactly what caused Dustin Clover to end up in prison. He was looking for someone to help him not be bored.

Being offered a job of selling dime bags of marijuana sounded like just the thing; it wouldn't be boring. How hard could that be? And he could make some big bucks. Of course, he would have to be careful; the cops kind of frown on this kind of business and his mom and dad would not like it either.

How exciting to a nine-year-old to be able to make his own cash. Kind of like playing hide and seek; you hide everything from mom and dad and the police, and seek those you would need to buy your product. Sounds like a fun game and Dustin played for nine years, until it abruptly stopped with facing a lot of time in prison.

God not only instructed me to write this book, but I also lived this with my nephew and his mom and dad. It's a heartbreaking walk along a treacherous down hill road.

It has been sixteen years since that scene in Court Room 3, and you as readers will hopefully see hope come into play as you step into this fascinating true story.

I do want to say I admire my sister, Jan, Dustin's mom. Many years have passed since she became a mother. She has provided for, cared for, protected, corrected and most of all, loved her children deeply. Having gone beyond, in hopes to offer each of them a good life.

Each child has a distinct set of rules. No two children are the same; she has three of her own so she knows this better than some do.

Raising children is not an easy task, but she persevered and held the course, and she still is. A mother is irreplaceable in every stage of their children's life.

Jan will always be the best mom she can with the help of God Almighty. I honor her for staying the course and trusting God to be her help during this storm. I love you, Sis.

Chapter 1

GOOD NAME IS TO BE CHOSEN

> Proverbs 22:1 (KJV) "A good name is to be chosen rather than great riches; Loving favor rather than silver and gold."

DO YOU THINK God gives names? I know he changed Saul's name to Paul. He named Jesus, and He named John. He changed Jacob's name to Israel. He named Solomon, He named Isaac. And there are many more. He knows our name.

These things are important enough for God to put instructions in His Word. Names are important, they tell a story of who we are and what we should become. A name will impact our children as they grow. A person's name is the greatest connection to their own identity and individuality. After meeting someone and they remember our name, we feel respected and more important. The above scripture is telling us to make sure we live up to the good name that was chosen. It is better than riches.

This baby was born March 9, 1986. Every mother knows with birth comes pain. My sister was having her third child and knew she would experience pain, but, for the most part, that pain dissipated when she held her sweet baby boy. She named him Dustin Caleb Clover. This means brave fighter, faithful, devotion, wholehearted, and bold. His Mom carried him nine months, loving him before he made his appearance. Now, life as it was for him inside his mom, no longer protected by her body, caused him to experience the pains of this life for himself. He had to learn to live outside of that protection. Babies are dependent on someone to care for them and as they grow and change, the self-part of them grows too, causing them to be even more demanding of their own way.

When Dustin was born things in our world had changed since my sisters and I were children. Our small town of Murphysboro, a town of now of 7,100 people, had plenty for kids to do when we were growing up. We had a nice park with a public swimming pool, a bowling alley, a roller-skating rink that became an ice-skating rink in the winter. There were two theaters, a drugstore fountain where you could get ice cream cones and ice cream drinks. The stores were open on main street until eight on Friday nights and our town was full of people then. We had basketball courts, a tennis court, and playgrounds for ball. If we didn't live near a playground, we made one out of an empty lot.

We lived in the same housing project as Dustin when we were kids. Parents were not afraid to let their kids roam the streets till dark. We knew when the streetlights came on we had better be in our own yard. But like I said, things were different back then.

The same housing project that we lived in is now called "The Hood." Why? The kids in the 1980s were encouraged to start selling drugs and Dustin became a product of that era. Not much left for kids to do in our small town, those days were gone. I am concerned that the future does not look favorable for things to improve.

Dustin, bored, and nine years of age got that encouragement to sell what he called "a dime bag of marijuana." This dime bag would cost the buyer $10.00. I am not sure what the seller had to pay for it or what their cut would have been. Whatever it was, it looked enticing to a nine-year-old and it was enough to carry on his lifestyle.

Remember the meaning of his name: brave, fighter, bold, faithful, devoted, wholehearted, a born leader, he just took the wrong road. Or did he? It was his decision, God just allowed him to experience it. God gives us the right to choose even though a nine-year-old should not be making decisions like this. He had outside influence and outside influences are not always a good thing and certainly should be supervised by a caring adult. In Dustin's case the adults were busy or simply blinded to the facts. This young man, even though around others, made his own decisions.

God has a way of directing our lives, not to harm us but to prosper us, to give us hope and a future. Like it says in Jeremiah 29:11. He knows those plans. Sometimes we have difficulty accepting God's way. When we look back on our years, we can see how he directed our path even though we fought it every step of the way. In Dustin's story, it is not just about his naive decision making, it includes those who ignored his cry for attention.

I was not involved with Dustin much when he was a little boy. But, I was the one who gave him his mullet haircut and every time he came to my house (where my salon was) he would ask, "Aunt Karen, you fix me pan-a-cakes?" So sweet, how could anyone turn that down? He had personality galore and such a cute way of saying things. He stayed with Granny Woosley (Jan and my mom) at times, and they would often walk past my house on their way to the park. Dustin would always stop and ask me to go along. He had such a sweet demeanor, and you would never think he would turn to the streets.

Often in our busy world the kids suffer more than we know.

Dustin's mom and dad both had to work, so he was with his older sisters often. As he grew, he got more involved with the kids in the area and found ways to get out of the house to meet up with them. He started to take drugs, smoke pot, as well as other things not suitable for a young boy. There were older men that influenced these boys; men that bought the liquor and the beer for these boys and girls. Dustin soon found himself wanting to make more money. The whirlwind in Dustin's young life continued to twist and turn and things started to seem like he was not in control. Like the meaning of his name, he decided to take on a leadership role around age twelve. He became very well known around Murphysboro, and in fact, Southern Illinois. All the hood kids knew who Dustin was, now known as "D Boy." He felt like a big man, he had made a name for himself. Important, even though being known for drug dealing was not a good thing in most people's eyes. To the gang members, you are the Man!

The things happening to Dustin back then were not visible to me. I am not sure about the rest of our family. I did know that my sister was at her wits end. She tried so hard to keep him out of trouble, always seeking help with those in authority on how to get him to change his path. After all, this was her baby and she wanted to protect him, even if it meant putting herself in harm's way.

D Boy. The name change was not for good. It was associated with drugs, lies, and evil; everything drawing him toward a path of destruction. Satan is running rampant trying his best to destroy our kids and families. D Boy was known, everyone knew him. Dustin was getting deeper and deeper into this pit, and even though he thought he was big stuff there was always someone higher up the ladder. Drug dealers from upstate were dead serious about their money. They pretended they cared about these kids; telling them they would be their big brother, showing them the way. In fact, this is exactly why Dustin joined the gang, "Gangster Disciples." He wanted to belong. The only way you could get into the gang was to show just how serious you are. Meaning you would take part in something that shows you took this position dead serious.

The things that these boys and girls would have to do did not prove anything except the fact it got them into even more trouble. I have listed things these kids would do showing how brave and fearless they were.

Before joining a gang, the gang leader would instruct them to do something like...Stealing something, beating up a random person, home invasion, fight with knives, steal guns, selling drugs, sexual acts. Things that would make you wonder why anyone would want to be in these gangs.

Listed here are reasons: low self-esteem, wanting to be important, a since of belonging, showing self-worth, and power.

Signs your child could be in gang involvement, and these could be as early as elementary school: experimenting with drugs, decline in school grades, unwillingness to attend family gatherings or share regular meals, change of friends, rebellious behavior, poor family bonding, keeping late hours, having large sums of money, gang graffiti in their bedrooms, gang clothes, hand signals to communicate with friends. We as parents need to be aware of our children's actions with these things. This kind of lifestyle mentioned is what brings on violence and stealing.

By the time Dustin was ten years old he was involved in gang activity by selling drugs; lesser amounts at first then came the bigger sales, until he was so deep into it there never seemed to be a way out.

No one ever thinks their kids would do this. My sister was no exception. We never want to believe this could happen to us.

IT HAPPENS!

Chapter 2

GOD IS WATCHING OVER YOU

> Psalm 121:5, 7-8 (NIV) "The LORD watches over you... The Lord will keep you from all harm, he will watch over your life; the Lord will watch over your coming and going both now and forevermore."

NOTHING HAPPENS IN our lives that God is not aware of. I do not care who you are. He knows each decision we all made and make. He even directs at different times. If something does not turn out like we think it should, it does not mean that is not the way it needed to happen for the finish to end well.

Think about this for a minute, have you had something happen that at the time did not look good, but turned out for the better? Suppose you are going to an event, you are running late, you are approaching a stop light and you pray it stays green, but it turns red. Now you must wait and the person in front of you takes their time going, when it turns green. Up ahead there was a major accident that could have included you if you had not had to wait. That was a God thing protecting you. You got up that morning and asked for His protection for the day. Instead of just being late you made the event, alive and well. Praise God.

We do not understand things that happen or the changes in our world. We all have experienced them, like growing up in our small-town years ago. Kids did not wonder what to do, we had many things to keep us occupied. Even living in the housing project was much like a commune, lots of kids to play with. Every evening we would play at the playground or got a ball game together for fun. Kids today do not seem to have an imagination anymore, with computers and tablets to keep them busy they hardly ever get out of the house.

It is no wonder, even in our small town that things got out of hand. We no longer have the things for kids to do. Little by little something was created for kids to do, and not the better choice. By the time Dustin was big enough to wander away from home, the kids he chose to hang out with were less than a desirable influence. The older kids took the younger ones and helped to guide them down the wrong road, getting them involved in things that caused them to stray even further away from family life. Gangs and drugs were becoming the new fun.

Family life has changed from when we were kids, no one sits down to family dinners anymore. Moms and Dads both working, kids watching kids, no family time, a lot of chaos.

God is never unaware of the things in our life. The scripture at the beginning of this chapter says He will watch over the coming and going now and forevermore. He knows what troubles us. Things happen to us because of decisions made for us. We did not have control over those things in our lives that caused us to get angry or be sad. Things like that just happen.

Divorce is one of those things; it is hard on kids, especially a kid that seems lost in the shuffle already. Loss of a loved one that is a hero will devastate a kid when he feels like his world is falling apart anyway. Both things happened to Dustin at a young age. Mom and dad divorcing was one thing but losing his older step-brother who looked as if he had everything going for him - good looks, great athlete, made good grades, was liked by everyone. Dustin's hero took his life, and it took Dustin down still yet another road. Anger rose in him, and he was out to do whatever he thought he was big enough to do. These things pushed him to not seem to care who he hurt.

Dustin, now called D Boy by all his friends, was out to make himself known. Every time he got himself in a tough situation, he knew his mom would get him out.

One incident he had gotten into was so serious that he thought other gang members were going to kill him. At this time cell phones were a part of our lives, so all he had to do was call his mom. He was whispering to her that he was in big trouble; he needed her to come to his rescue. She drove to where he was and found herself in the middle of a dire situation. Dustin jumped out of where he was and got into her car and they drove away. Now these gang members are not respecters of persons. God true to His promise protected them. A mother who thinks her son might be killed will do whatever she has to do to protect. This mom always did, it did not matter what it was, she had no fear when it came to her son's protection. Like a Momma Bear.

Dustin at an early age figured this out and depended on his mom to be his hero. This way of life seemed to be working good for Dustin, until his mom met Donnie and they decided to get married.

Donnie with two children and Jan with Dustin. It is a known fact that putting two families together is not an easy task. First, it is not what God intended to be, though many of us have tried. Second, if the children of the two people do not want this to happen, they can make it most difficult causing major strife for the couple. Even being rooted with God the trials make it difficult for that marriage to hold up. It takes work.

Dustin was sixteen now and thought he was a man, except for the need of his mom to save him now and again. He had his mom wrapped up in his life and this marriage made it a challenge to be able to stay connected. Because of the situation Dustin moved out of his mom's house and went to live with his girlfriend and her dad. With no one to hold him accountable he ended up quitting school, and shortly after enrolled in a rebound program that was never completed. The household he was living in was less than desirable. Dustin told me that the girlfriend's Dad sold weed and Cocaine. A sixteen-year-old in that environment to make anyone happy is not the right road to take. But Jan thought she was doing the best for all and honestly, Dustin was wearing her out. She really did not know what to do but did her best to keep peace in the family.

Donnie was an over the road truck driver and when he was gone Dustin could come to the house and bring his laundry but until Donnie was gone Dustin could not step foot into is Mom's house. This broke my heart. I had experienced some of a comparable situation in my own life with my son, and it hurts to know your child, no matter how old they are, is not wanted. I know there is such a thing as tough love, but so extremely hard to do especially for a mom. Dads can do this sort of thing easier or so it seems.

Dustin continued his lifestyle which included drugs, gangs, girls, and all that went along with it. He went to church with his mom, but trying to live two different lifestyles just was not working.

Sixteen, living on his own, and hanging out with a rough crowd, out all night, sleeping during the day, does not lead to a healthy life. It spells trouble. Quick money and parties all lead to more of the same. Big trouble!

I will never forget the phone call for prayer, in the early hour of the morning eighteen years ago. My sister had heard on the scanner, there had been a shooting in Bridgewood, another housing project near to where Dustin had grown up, this time things had worsened. A kid had been shot and the police were looking for two white male suspects. Dustin Clover was one of them.

The officers were notified by Herrin police that the vehicle they were looking for was in their city. Dustin's oldest sister resided there with her family. Dustin and the other kid did go there but were not in Jana's house. The police did not believe Jana when she told them Dustin was not there. They arrested Jana saying she was hiding her brother and took her to jail. More grief for a mother.

Dustin and the other kid were long gone from Jana's but apprehended in West Frankfort, a small town northeast of Herrin, Illinois. They stopped to get something to eat, thinking they were far enough away from the police.

Next stop Jackson County Jail.

Not new to a prayer life, I began to pray for Gods will. God has a plan for each of us and He loves us enough to carry it out even if we resist. His word says this in Jeremiah 29:11 (NIV) "'For I know the plans I have for you,' declares the LORD, 'plans to prosper you and not to harm you, plans to give you hope and a future.'" I am very certain if I quoted this scripture to Dustin, it would not seem that God was going to prosper him and not harm him, and hope? I am sure he did not see hope. Here he sat behind bars not knowing if mom could get him out of this mess. Incarceration had never been a part of his plan, but he had faith his mom would get him out. That was his hope.

His Mom had always worked hard to keep him and all her family out of trouble, hadn't she?

Chapter 3

DOUBLE TROUBLE

Proverbs 10:9 (NIV) "The man of integrity walks securely, but he who takes a crooked path will be found out."

DUSTIN AND ANOTHER young man approached the area in their vehicle where the drug deal was to take place. Their contacts came out of the shadows. Dustin saw one of the boys pull a gun. He had no alternative but to draw his gun and fire. The kids involved with street life and the drug scene are instructed - if a person pulls a gun, you had better be ready and act immediately, otherwise you may not be able to.

The kids that are involved in gangs play games on their Gameboys and Xbox. It is much like training. These games are examples for acting out real life instances. It is where they get their ideas for a way of living. Not a good practice and gets them into trouble, often more than once.

Shots rang out, not unusual for Bridgewood. The police received a phone call from the hospital that they had a gun shot victim and that Dustin was involved. In a matter of minutes they were in pursuit of Dustin and his friend. Hearing this incident on a police scanner, my sister called me for prayer. The boys? Arrested in West Frankfort, Illinois. Not far enough away from Murphysboro to be what they called, safe.

It was a very frightening time for those of us who were hoping desperately that it was not Dustin, and that the young man who had drawn the gun would be okay. Prayers for that young man's life had been initiated, and he lived! Praise God! In a noticeably short amount of time, he was back on the street waiting for the opportunity to retaliate. He had not learned from this; if anything, his actions had worsened. But our family and I are sure his family was grateful he was alive and well.

Dustin got his fill of County jail and did not like it one little bit. He kept telling his mom, "You got to get me out of here." And that is exactly what she and his father did.

Jan had already been down this road with Dustin's dad, David. Before Dustin was born, David had gotten himself into trouble, a federal case. Being married, she already had a taste of having to deal with the law and prison time. Now she was facing it again with her son.

So much of the time children manage to follow in the footprints of their parents. Dustin had heard all the past stories about his dad and his cousins. This family had to uphold their name, be tough, stand tall; even if they got caught doing the things that should have been left alone. David had served two years in a federal camp, but my sister can tell you the loved one is not the only one to do the time. She had to constantly stay connected from the outside so he could be safe on the inside. Fighting the system is not a fun thing to do. By the time David could come home Jan had had her fill of our judicial system. Thank God for His faithfulness and His protection and provision for her family. I do believe Dustin's dad learned one thing from being in prison, and that is he did not want to go back. His lifestyle has not changed much to this day, but he knows with being older, physical fighting is out of the question. He has mellowed.

Knowing what they had been through during David's prison time, Jan and he felt they had to do something to help their son. The bond was set for $100,000.00, which meant it would take $10,000.00 to get him out on bail. Bond money will be returned if the person shows up for court, less a percentage taken for court cost.

Once the bond money was paid and Dustin was released, he could not stay at his mom's, so he moved in with my husband and me. We were happy to take Dustin in our home and did what we could to make him as comfortable as possible in trying to make a home for him. He needed spending money, so we gave him odd jobs to do around our house until he found a job. He worked with my husband on our deck and stained our fence. We encouraged him to have a friend over to swim and his girlfriend was welcome to visit. I continued to show him I trusted him, I even let him take my car to detail it for me. We went to a family reunion in Kentucky and while we were there, we rented a jet ski so he and his girlfriend could take it out on the lake. I wanted him to know I trusted him. Not often but sometimes he would let me cook for him. I found out he liked chocolate chip cookie dough, so I kept that in the refrigerator, and he liked my grilled cheese sandwiches. But he really wanted fast food. Eating at one of the drive-up places kept him on the run, always on the move. He did not want to get caught with his guard down.

Dustin got a job at a local restaurant just down the street from where we lived. I would go pick him up when his shift was over. He liked his job; I know from experience that liking your job makes going to work much easier. I was beginning to see hope where he was concerned. This restaurant was close enough to walk, but I was concerned for him since there were those out on the street to retaliate. Dustin did tell me he came face to face with a kid one night, but because of the audience, he only spouted off a warning that he was after Dustin. Nothing ever became of that.

He was with us all summer and fall and I had been working on trying to get him into Teen Challenge, a program for young people to overcome drug abuse and set their life straight. Another sister and I were willing to put up the money up for him to go. All we needed now was for the Judge to say he could go. I was feeling positive about this becoming a reality.

It was Friday evening, October 8; Dustin's court date was Monday, October 11. He came home with two guys I had never met and told me he was going to go with them and would not be home that night. I warned him and reminded him of his court date on Monday. Expressing that I did not think this was a great plan, I was in hopes that he would reconsider. He had come too far to ruin all he had accomplished the past summer. He assured me it would be okay. One of the guys was telling me he worked with his grandpa as a carpenter. The name of the business was Building for Jesus. I had seen that van around town, so I knew the business was for real, but you just know when something does not feel right. This young man was working too hard to convince me that he was a good person; I felt like the snake would strike any minute. I could not talk Dustin out of it, and it was his decision to make.

It was just after midnight, another call this time from my daughter wanting to know if Dustin was at home. And, of course, he was not. I called Jan this time and told her I did not know what was happening, but I knew Dustin was involved. She and her husband had separated; she was in the throes of trying to figure out why her husband was acting so strange. She did not know at this time that he had a brain tumor.

It turns out the young men that Dustin was with were involved in getting guns in a small town southwest of Murphysboro. When they came back with their bounty, they went to the boy's house that had said he worked for his grandpa. They started to party, drinking, and popping pills. This, with course talk, gave these boys a bogus confidence.

A third boy sporting a sawed-off shotgun and Dustin with a twenty-two semi-automatic, decided to go to a woman's house to collect drug money. When she told them she did not have his money, another person at her residence saw that the kid with Dustin had a gun and called the police. It did not take long for the police to show up. When the sirens and lights started showing up the kid with the sawed-off shotgun fired it and ran toward the main street. Police were everywhere and apprehended this kid. Dustin went into the woman's house that they were doing drug business with, there were two other people in the house. Dustin meant them no harm only trying to escape from the police.

The police now had the place surrounded. In his mind's eye he could still escape. He went out the back, stayed in the shadows and tried to make a break. One of the police officers tackled him just around the corner that he thought would lead to freedom. One by one the police were taking their turn hitting him. Dustin did have a gun and did not hand it over. When they finally got the gun out of his hand, they continued to hit him, and before they took him to jail, the police took him to the hospital. He had to have several staples above his left eye.

During my call to Jan, she asked me if I thought she should go to where the police had Dustin surrounded and I told her it might make matters worse. That night was another night that seemed forever long. Again, prayer time for my nephew, do we ever stop praying for our kids? God has never failed me. If anyone fails, it is us. I had to continue to trust in a God who loves us.

I met Jan at the county jail the next morning after she had seen him so beat up. He had a seizure and she had to leave. We waited long hours in the parking lot constantly checking to see if we could visit. The ones in authority would only let his mom in. When she saw him this time, she flat out lost it! We figured out why they were so reluctant to let us in to see Dustin. His eyes were swollen shut, the gash stapled over his left eye, and he had not been cleaned up from the police beating from the night before when he was arrested.

I know the adrenalin was flowing and I also know not all police are cruel. Dustin did have a gun, and that gun had to be removed from Dustin's possession. The police had to do their job. When Dustin arrived at County jail, they stripped him down and put him in a very cold room; we were grateful that God was watching over him, because this could have turned out far worse. I have been around police work since I was in my early twenties, was married to a police officer once and I was appalled that a kid would be beat this bad and by so many. There was more to this escapade than met the eye.

Since Dustin was twelve, he had been able to slide through law enforcement fingers. In every situation, if he did not do it on his own, his mom got him out of situations. But until now, no guns had been a part of his trouble with the law, everything to this point had been drug sales or traffic offences and nothing cut and dried. You might think, drug sales? There is always a reason for one to turn their head. In today's world you do not have to look far to find that those in authority could be as corrupt and lawless as the person being arrested.

Now, they had D Boy. Going before the judge, the bond was set at $1,000,000.00. It would take $100,000.00 to get him out. This time he was not going anywhere. At nineteen years of age God was telling us, "Not this time." I believe God was saying, "I have plans for this young man, it is time you put him in My hands."

There was a new chapter in Dustin's life. He was in County Jail for several months; he opted for a Jury trial.

Chapter 4

NEVER-ENDING TRIAL

Proverbs 3:5-6 (NIV) "Trust in the Lord with all your heart and lean not to your own understanding. In all your ways submit to Him, and he will make your path straight."

THEY DID NOT start choosing a Jury until December 11. Dustin was arrested on October 8. He had healed up from the beating he took, any way mostly. He still had scars, headaches, and eye problems.

We totally had to trust God through this entire trial. Sitting in the court room waiting on the Judge to enter seemed like an eternity. I know Jan was heartbroken that her son was in more trouble than even could be imagined. He was so close to being able to go to Teen Challenge and now all we could do was turn him over to God's care. Only God knew what it would take for Dustin to commit to Him.

Dustin did share with me later that if he had been able to go to Teen Challenge he was planning to run and not do the program. Knowing that, I now could understand why the second round of trouble.

"All rise!" The Judge entered the court room and everyone stood in respect of his position. The two attorneys approached the bench and Dustin realized he had made a huge mistake.

"December 11, 2006
State of Illinois: Plaintiff
Dustin C. Clover: Defendant
Jury Trial"

There are 145 pages in the report of choosing this Jury. Seemed like it took forever, but a Jury was chosen.

The Plaintiff began....

Dustin was not a stranger in this court room. Unfortunately, he was only two days from concluding the first case. Now he finds himself back before a judge who had told him, "Do not come before me again!"

October 8, is when Dustin and his cohorts were arrested. October 11, was when the first case was to be concluded. Now, the only thing that can be brought up about the first case is the time that would be served. Nothing about the first case at this point could be addressed during the second case.

The trial did not end when they sentenced Dustin to forty-eight total years for this second case. He has lived every minute, day after day from that moment on. It took the very breath out of him. Stunned he looked at his mother in disbelief. He hadn't killed anyone. This was like living in the twilight zone. Nineteen years of age and looking at forty-eight years incarcerated. He thought his mom could do anything, and she tried. His thoughts turned to when he was a little boy; God was reminding him of when he went to church, and when he was baptized, and loved Jesus. Walking away was not part of the commitment. When he was nine years old and did not take a stand for Jesus and walked the other way - now, look where he was, what he was facing.

Jan worked hours going over all the transcripts of her son's case. She was a believer and prayed and spiritually fought the battle. The hard part for this mom was releasing her son into God's hands so He could work in Dustin's life. God was not going to let go of Dustin. His Mom hanging on to him, and trying to fix, only prolonged the situation. This is like the analogy of the little boy who took the broken toy to his father to fix. After watching Daddy work on the toy for a moment, he thought he could take it and finish fixing it; but found out he could not fix it. So much of the time we cannot let go and let God.

In the middle of the trial, my sister had to go to a St. Louis Hospital because her husband was dying of a brain tumor. They did surgery, but it was not long before they sent him home to die. God must have given her the strength to carry on. It seemed like everything was crashing in all at the same time.

> Psalm 46:1-3 (NIV) "God is our refuge and strength, an ever-present help in trouble. Therefore, we will not fear, though the earth gives way, and the mountains fall into the heart of the sea, though its waters roar and

foam and the mountains quake with their surging."

We must TRUST in a Living God.

Until a person wants to submit to God, it is a real struggle. Dustin's mom and I tried our absolute best to encourage him. I sent him a study Bible, along with devotions; I wrote to him faithfully and visited monthly. His Mom would not miss a visit no matter where he was we would travel to see him. Thankfully, it was not so far that it was an overnight stay.

Fighting the fight of faith, Dustin finally got it. It took approximately five years for him to make the best out of a bad situation. That Judge got his attention when he said forty-eight years incarceration. That did not include the thirteen for his first case.

Dustin was locked up with the same people who walked the same road he did. If it were not for the ones who had given their heart to God, the battle would have been much harder, and harder for us to communicate that things would turn out for the best. Thankfully, Dustin and I started having "God word" time in our visits. I could see a real change in him and not the superficial one that had been put on display for the last five years. That was a long time coming, but it did come and I for one was very thankful.

Jan continued to work on getting someone to read all the trial transcripts in hopes to find a loophole. I came across a few while I was refreshing myself with the information to write these truths.

One loophole is as follows. The gun that was in Dustin's possession that night never had batteries in the laser. The expert witness said, "The gun was a twenty-two automatic with a laser attached and still had ammo in the magazine." When arrested, each witness said, "Dustin was repeatedly clicking the trigger." If that were so and there were bullets in the magazine, that gun would have been firing and someone would have been hurt. Also, the entire case was built on the fact that the laser (which had no batteries) was being used. The laser on the gun when working correctly would give the shooter a better shot at his target. This could not happen since there were no batteries in the laser of this gun. I was in that court room for every portion of the trial and listened very intently. I could not believe Dustin's attorney did not follow up on that. Another witness stated she saw Dustin fire his gun at a police officer with the laser working. This again could not happen. Later the woman, who was the same woman doing drug business with Dustin and the other boy, admitted that she lied. She had said this because the police had threatened her. She admittedly said she was a drug addict and kept saying she was high when the police officer was questioning her. She recanted her testimony; stating on tape that she had lied. None of this evidence helped in trying to get time back for Dustin.

With no batteries in the laser, the laser would not work. The batteries that would have been in the gun's laser would have been held in by screws. The expert witness was asked if there were screws in the gun's laser, he answered yes, the screws were there but no batteries.

This was taken to the appellate court to no avail.

I asked myself, why couldn't they see this? It is as plain as the nose on your face. I believe it was because it was not time for Dustin to come out of this place. God took everybody's hand off because He had Dustin's attention.

Like Paul or Timothy or John in the Bible, life even then, was busy, and people are distracted by the world. Some would say but those men were doing God's work. And I would say, yes, that is correct and especially important work writing God's word. They needed solitude and undivided attention. I believe if Dustin could have sat still and known that God wanted to use him and he was open to God, great things could have transpired. And still might. He has learned a great deal in his sixteen years incarcerated and I might say with all that has happened he has become a wonderful adult.

Paul may have not written four of the books in the New Testament had he not been in prison. John wrote John, First, Second & Third John, and Revelation. Both men were imprisoned for preaching the gospel. John was exiled to the Island of Patmos, as a result of anti-Christian persecution under a Roman Emperor. We today are grateful that these men were obedient to God. Prison life could have not been easy back in those days, but it did give a time of solitude for writing, thanks be to God for His word.

Chapter 5

LIFE BEHIND THE WALLS

James 1:14-15 (NKJV) "But each one is tempted when he is drawn away by his own desires and enticed. Then, when desire has conceived, it gives birth to sin, when it is full grown, brings forth death."

DUSTIN GOT FORTY-EIGHT years for his second case; with good behavior he will serve twenty-one years. The years he has already served have not been easy. He first had to figure out how to live and accept orders in this newfound lifestyle. He now is on a schedule: when to get up, when to go to bed, when to eat, what to eat, when to take a shower and to only be able to be outside once maybe twice a day. The rest of the time is spent in the cell, a small area shared with another person, a person not of your choosing. Bunk beds, no air-conditioning. If you have a family to provide for you, you can have a fan, small TV with no remote. Everyone gets a box to keep their personal supplies in like packaged foods and toiletries. You can go to the store to buy extras if you have money on your books. The cost is ridiculous depending on the facility. An inmate can have up to five visits a month; usually four-hour visits on a hard stool. The rules for all prisons are not the same but, it seemed to me when I visited, everyone in the visiting room was polite and respectful. I have determined the ones incarcerated, once off drugs, can do very well for themselves provided they have family to help and stay connected with.

I would ask Dustin how things were there, and he would say, "Okay for the most part." So, as time went on Dustin could see that having a job and going to school and yes, going to Church, was going to be beneficial. The first thing he signed up for was to go to Church. But not everyone that went to church was there to worship or learn about God. The gangs figured out they could meet there so they could communicate things they wanted to do. Dustin at this point in his life really was interested in learning and he met helpful people in Church.

Sometimes it is necessary to move to another facility, again, every prison is different and when there is a need to be moved to another facility, he has to learn all the new rules again. I found that out even with our visits. One reason for a move would be someone wanting to always pick a fight; you cannot back down from this behavior, because if those people detect fear, they really will pick on you. Dustin knows he has to stand up, but he is smart enough to know when it is time to move on. Another reason would be to work in the industry. If you have done all you can do at one facility you can make a move to better, yourself. Things he has learned while incarcerated: welding, plumbing, working in the officers' quarters, filing, one of the best jobs was dog training. These jobs keep him busy and when he does have free time it is out in the yard or the activity room to work out.

I asked him if he ever played ball or basketball and he told me no, because of those who were quick to fight. I thought that was smart on his part. One thing he did do was finish his high school education in prison but not through their program. He shared with me that you had to live in a different house and the inmates in that house were too noisy. He got his diploma by doing his studies though the mail. The classes which included a Bible course not only got him a diploma but helped him tremendously with his relationship with God and knowing His word. This personal relationship with God was the very thing that was going to get him through this challenge he was facing. The original trial opened the door for Dustin to experience the trial that brought and continues to bring him through the fire and not get burned.

Dustin started to write poems. The first poem he wrote was, "Look At Me Now." When I read this, I knew this would be the title of this book. I have shared this poem along with others in this book. Each poem depicts where he was at the time of writing, some poems are sad, but you can always read that this young man had come to a relationship with God Almighty.

The first five years were the hardest for Dustin. He had indeed been drawn away by his own desires and enticed, and it took at least five years to understand that. God was not going to let go of him. Thankfully, Dustin had not lost his life to death but lost his life of living in the years he was walking and living according to his own desires. Even though incarcerated with the type of people that helped get him in this mess, he now had to separate himself from them. Separating from those people was not hard; in fact, he wondered how he ever was able to communicate with them at all. Of course, he was no longer on anything to make that happen. Drugs will destroy your life. Only when God takes the wheel and becomes the driver of your life, will you be able to give up drugs entirely. However, God does not just take the wheel; we must give it to Him. He gives us free will and we have to make the choice to give it to Him and to leave it with Him. He wants us to relinquish the bad in our lives so He can bring out the good. For the last sixteen years, Dustin has had to live with and in the middle of the same world that brought him to prison, with the exception that prison is supposed to be structured. Not everyone thinks "structured" when prison is mentioned. Dustin no longer had the freedom to come and go as he pleased, instead of a nice clean home with tasty food and nice clothes, he had a bed with a box and a roommate that may be clean or not. Still yet he had to live among the same people he had lived with and got into trouble with. Having to deal with daily life issues and learn to resist allowing anyone to get him into trouble. He had to learn who to be friends with and trust. This takes skill and always being alert, not just for the inmates but also those in authority. Again, we have free will, and must make good choices; you either want to stay out of trouble, and do your time, or do your time and when you come out of there go back to making the same mistakes. Statistics show the latter.

Dustin chose to change and stay away from those who would try their best to make trouble. I am certain his mom and dad and yes, Aunt Karen, were glad he was working toward bettering himself to be able to come out of prison with his head held high, knowing he had used these years to educate himself and should be able to get a job, and still be young enough to have a family. This is his desire.

Chapter 6

FROM BOY TO MAN

II Corinthians 5:17 (NKJV) "Therefore, if anyone is in Christ, he is a new creation; old things have passed away; behold, all things have become new."

ARRESTED AT AGE eighteen, enters the prison system at age twenty. He is now thirty-five and has matured while in prison. I would hate to think what might have happened to him had he not gotten help. God is good and because we can look back over the last sixteen years and be sorry for him having to have to live all his young adulthood in prison, he was in the lesser of the two evil places. The world Dustin was living in without God was spiraling downward fast, and it took God to stop it so this young man could live.

In prison he has come to really have a personal relationship with God his Savior. Even though it is hard to say, Dustin has come a long way and I pray he will continue down this road once he completes his payment to society for the wrongs he did. But now praise God he is free in his spirit. I believe Dustin will come out of prison as a new creation like the Scripture says. Old things have passed away and new things have come. I love this young man like he was my own and if his life had not taken this turn, I would not have gotten to know him and now we have a great relationship.

God's ways are higher than ours and even though we would love for Dustin to be able to come home we know God's timing is perfect. Dustin has accomplished things that would have cost a great deal of money had he pursued them outside of those walls.

#1 A Bible study course bringing him to have a personal relationship with our loving Savior.

#2 A diploma causing him to be proud to show he finished his high school education.

#3 Taking college classes.

#4 Learning the trade of plumbing and worked at this job.

#5 Another trade, welding and worked at this job. He made his Grandpa Dewey proud, because that was his trade. They would often discuss welding when I could take his grandpa to see him.

#6 Dog training and worked this job. This is I believe his most favorite, it was something he could hug and love.

#7 He writes poetry, and one poem was published. Others written are on life experiences while in prison.

#8 Office job. Filing important papers and organizing.

#9 This last year, he took up painting with acrylics. So, he added another form of art.

He learned how to rely on God and stay out of trouble. He also learned not everyone who says they are your friend, is your friend.

He now has a better relationship with his mom and his family.

He lost both of his grandparents while incarcerated but, Granny and Grandpa were able to visit him several times.

So much learned and I believe he will put it to practice. He is still working toward getting time taken off his sentence by getting jobs and schooling and staying out of trouble. Not an easy road to travel in the world let alone prison.

So much has changed in the prison system. There are more opportunities to better yourself for the day that you can return to society. My nephew has hope of having a place of his own with a family. This shows maturity and I believe he will achieve what he desires by working hard to get it and trusting God to provide it.

Because Dustin has such a wonderful personality, he makes friends easily, guards take to Dustin. People are never put in your life without a purpose for being there. All of those who friended Dustin helped him over these years, needs were met. I visited each month, and each visit I could tell the ones that were genuine friends to Dustin. You must be careful choosing friends, no matter where life takes you, but in prison it could cause friction within those walls. It is good however to know people like you and trust you. It reminds me of Joseph when Potiphar, an officer of Pharaoh, gave him second position in his household. Joseph honored that position even when Potiphar's wife tried to get him to be with her. When he turned her down, she set him up and he lost that position and was put back in prison. That must have been extremely hard to swallow when you do right and end up going to prison for it. But in this case, it was the king's prison. What looked bad again for Joseph ended up good for him. Joseph accurately interpreted the dreams of two prisoners, but the chief cupbearer did not remember him and forgot him in prison for two years, until Joseph was given the opportunity to interpret Pharaoh's dream. This led to Pharaoh putting Joseph, then thirty years old, over all the land of Egypt, second only to Pharaoh himself. (Genesis 41:40-41) If God be for you who can stand against you? Dustin continues to make friends. Having people in your life is very important.

    I remember one guy kept trying to get Dustin's attention; this was around the time when he was beginning his relationship with God. This man kept telling Dustin he needed to talk to him, and he would quote scripture to Dustin. Dustin in turn asked me if I thought he was on the up and up. As it turned out he too was a big help to Dustin. God will put people in your life if only for a season. It is a good thing. Like when the Eunuch, traveling back home, was reading in the book of Isaiah. The Eunuch did not understand what he was reading and wanted to know who Isaiah was writing about. The scripture was talking about Jesus coming and dying for us. So Philip, traveling on the same road, arrived and sat next to the Eunuch and helped him understand what he was reading, and ended up baptizing him. The Spirit of the Living God told Philip to go to this Eunuch. God knew this man needed help and Philip lead this Eunuch to Christ. People need people. Over the years, the right people have been in Dustin's life; people to stay in his life and people just for a time. Dustin has found life with its negatives brings pain, and out of pain comes purpose.

We must empty out the negative and make room for what God has for us. The fruit of the Spirit is love, joy, peace, patience, goodness, faithfulness, kindness, gentleness, and self-control. This gives us health, youth, joy unspeakable and full of glory. This on its own will grow you up, and can be real for everyone. God will draw you and it will get stronger like two magnets connecting. Pay attention, Satan draws as well. Resist Satan and he will flee. God's drawing is not only for you, but for you to now reach out to others and help them too. When we open ourselves to God by dumping the negative, God can fill you up; you will grow leaps and bounds. My prayer is for Dustin to realize that he is in a place where he can help these people come to God. Now this is what will change a boy to a man.

Chapter 7

CHANGES WERE MADE

> Psalm 27:11 (NIV) "Teach me your way, Lord; lead me in a straight path because of my oppressors."

WHEN DUSTIN MADE the decision to let God direct his life, I could tell he was more at peace with what had happened to him. Because of the decisions he made without God, he ended up at the very bottom of the pit, looking up was the only option. God will use trials to train us to do better. Then instead of making more major bad decisions we now ask the Holy Spirit to help us.

It seems when we start to experience God's peace in our lives, we cannot always accept that peace that passes all understanding. We will enjoy it for a moment, and then we wonder why I am not worried about my situation? If we are not careful Satan will steal that joy away. Dustin had to call out to God through these years to regain the peace that only God can give. He found that by getting a job, going to school, and simply helping someone else were the things that made him happy. The more he called out to God the better things seemed to be.

God's word instructs us to resist the Devil and he will flee from us and undoubtedly Satan does not want us to continue at rest. It is his job to cause unrest. Dustin had to always be on guard. In a place where evil runs rampant, the ones who would not like you to succeed will certainly try their best to interfere by starting trouble. There were times when Dustin had to stand up for himself; he could not cower in a place like that. Showing the troublemakers you are not afraid will cause them to back up. Why? Partially because he already had his training on the streets. They call it "being street wise," but mostly because God was on his side and the angel armies are always there to protect.

Sixteen years is a long time to fight this battle, Dustin did not kill anyone. The main reason for his prison stay was drugs, gangs, and having a gun in his possession. His youth was taken away from him, now he has to make the best of this world he finds himself in.

If I were to ask Dustin this question "What would you tell the kids of today about the choices they are making?" This would be his answer. "If I could tell these kids one thing about my life, it would be that I wish I would have listened to my parents. At eighteen years old, I have a total of sixty-one years for both offences in prison. I did everything from doing drugs, selling drugs and guns, caught up in the gangs/street lifestyle. All my so-called homies that I thought would be by my side, no matter what, acted like I was dead. And some told on me to save themselves. These are people I would have given my life for or killed for. At the end of the day my mother, father, aunt, and family are the ones by my side. I lived that life and if what

I have gone through can change the path of one life, then it was all worth it. Trust me; this is not an easy ride! Be careful of the friends you choose. Real friends are hard to come by! That life was not worth all the pain and trouble I caused myself and loved ones. I always thought I was only hurting myself but that was not the case. Everyone who stands next to me is hurting as well and having to deal with all of this. You may get away with that life and the things you do for a month, a year, maybe even several years, but eventually you will get caught. I wish I would have taken a different route because this is no life to live. Part of change is changing the ones you run with. Please take my advice. The system does not care to take your life away for several years and in my case a lot of years."

This young man has spent sixteen years of his life behind bars. Trust me and him when we say, "He knows!" Dustin has written poems concerning his day-to-day life and the struggles and his change when God put that change in his heart. Nothing made me, his aunt, any happier than the fact that I could see that change. He started asking me questions about the Bible and I was so grateful to witness the change in this incredible young man. He has worked hard to better himself. But God blessed him with a new heart. Create in me a new heart O God and renew a right spirit within me.

Changes continually are made. Dustin has reached out to different guys to encourage them to make the change in their life. One person he told me about was David. David claimed to be an atheist. He would call Dustin a Bible thumper, but that did not stop Dustin from trying to talk to him. Over and over, he would tell Dustin, "Do not try and push your beliefs on me." As a joke, and trying to keep it light, still trying to witness to him, Dustin would slide Bible pamphlets from church under his door. Dustin and David worked together in the industry at Shawnee Correctional Center, they were friends. When David became sick with cancer nine months before he was going to be able to go home, he became scared and upset. Dustin asked him if he could pray with him, and he allowed Dustin to pray with him. David accepted Christ into his life before he passed. There are several that Dustin led to Christ; two of them knew Dustin from before he went to prison and saw the difference in him. Our lives lived before someone speaks volumes. We should be Gods open word before people. Dustin's change was evident, and that change made others want what he had, they needed to change. God used Dustin's situation to change the hearts of not only a dying man but also some who still needed to live and be a witness to others.

Chapter 8

KEEPING UP THE PACE

> Joshua 1:5-6 (ESV) "No man shall be able to stand before you all the days of your life. As I was with Moses, so I will be with you. I will not leave you or forsake you. Be strong and courageous…"

LIFE BEHIND THESE walls can only be told by the ones living it. Dustin on a regular basis wrote his feelings down in the form of poetry. In November 2019 Dustin wrote this poem:

KEEP UP THE PACE

Laying in bed staring at the wall,
watching in my mind everything around me fall.
Its dark I can't see,
why God this can't be
Hell is hot, no where cold,
61 years because I wouldn't fold!
Now that's hard to take,

especially when all the ones you thought was true just turned out to be fake.
Is this some type of mistake?
Shaking my head, my stomach is turning,
I feel a fire inside something is burning.
Where are all the ones who said they were true,
still living their lives as there is nothing to do?
Sometimes questioning in everything I believe in, was it real.
Still to this day sometimes I'm not sure how I feel.
I know they say God is the way,
I read my bible verses and I pray every day
I try to be a good example and live what's preached,
even though I question on what some teach.
At the end of the day I'm playing my hand that was dealt,
because of my poor choices under my belt.
Trust me I'm no saint,
but be careful of the picture you decide to paint
That picture can be easily be painted about you,
then what would you decide to do
Oh breathing is heavy u can't take a breath,
when you picture all you have left
My 19-30's gone down the drain
still pushing through but nowhere the same. I'm almost there I can see the light
PLEASE GOD help me to not give up the fight
I fight, I fall, I pray, I crawl, I swing, I punch, I get ate for lunch through this roller coaster
Behind this prison wall
Hearing all these souls scream, as they need Gods call.

Keeping Up The Pace

Sometimes He answers other times you wonder where He's at,
but I'm gonna keep beating at that door even if I've gotta hit it with a bat.
God can you hear me? I've been screaming out loud,
why aren't you answering as I peak through the cloud
I can hear you loud and clear, when you whisper or just think, even when you shed a tear I see you my son I haven't forgot,
all these years you've prayed a lot
Struggled and fought, seems like your life was done,
I've protected you, your life has just begun.
Don't give in you are at the end of your race.
Take a deep breathe and keep up the pace.

By Dustin Clover 11-12-2019

Every day is a challenge for Dustin. Some days are very dark, given the atmosphere within those walls. Nothing is too big or too small for God. He will always show up at just the right moment. Even in the lives of those of us having to bear the trauma of the outside world.

    Joshua had a noticeably big job ahead of him. After Moses died, more than two million people were to be led into a strange new land. So, God told Joshua he would be with him just like he was with Moses. Telling him to be strong and of good courage. That is what God tells us today. He will always be with us and we are to be strong and courageous. Every new venture is a challenge and without God it can be frightening. With God it can be a great adventure. Every day we face new challenges; we may not conquer nations but we face tough situations, difficult people, and temptations. God promises He will never abandon us or fail to help us. Ask God and conquer life's challenges with Him.

Stronger each day if we draw near to God. Looking back at Moses and his challenges makes you wonder how the Israelites could ever have had their focus on anything but God and His marvelous mercy. His mercies are new every morning. God provided daily for the Israelites, and He will do it repeatedly for all of us. Then, now, and always. He will watch over those He loves and provide for our every need. He wants us to live a vibrant life in his light, being ever aware of his presence. Dustin year after year fills his mind with formidable scriptures to encourage himself knowing God is Love and He wants us to know our challenges are nothing for Him, because He is a mighty fortress and our refuge; a very present help in time of trouble. He bids us to come to him, all who are weary and burdened and He will give us rest. (Matthew 11:28) Even accepting the rest He provides is hard to understand. But, in my thirty-five years of serving Him, I realize when your focus is on Jesus you are at rest, and when you listen to His voice, that still small voice adds rest to your very soul.

When you know you are walking with Him it does not matter where He leads you. We have come to trust Him and feel safe. Dustin feels God's presence in this manner and there is nothing like that peace that passes all understanding, a time of rest. While you are basking in His rest and peace, that is when His joy floods over you like when the rainfalls on parched ground.

Psalm 132:14 (KJV) "This is my rest for ever: here will I dwell; for I have desired it."

When you have gone through what seems like years of trials and challenges, we are ready and desire God's rest. He will not forget us. He sees the struggle and His word will encourage you to believe; your life has just begun. It is not over. God will use those who believe and trust in Him. So, "Keep Up The Pace."

Chapter 9

The Ups and Downs

> Matthew 6:33 (ESV) "But seek first the kingdom of God and his righteousness, and all these things will be added to you."

THE POEMS THAT Dustin writes tell the story of his life behind these walls he endures daily. I was only given a few, but I am sure if we had all of them, we would see the ups and downs of his life for the past sixteen years. We see those times in his life where he allowed his mind to wander and allowed Satan to play havoc with him. When we allow it, our minds will carry us away. Satan likes very much to get into your head, but we have it built into us to survive. We will not go through life without trouble and as soon as we realize what is happening, we can stop the work of the Devil. The way you do that is to first acknowledge you are being tormented, next lift your hands and shout Hallelujah! That my friends, is the highest praise to our God and He will fight for you!

> Jeremiah 31:3-4 (NIV) says, "I have loved you with an everlasting love. I have drawn

you with unfailing kindness I will build you up again and you will be rebuilt. God will take your brokenness and build you up new."

Psalm 30:5 (NKJV) says, "Weeping may endure for a night but, joy comes in the morning."

Life is an up-and-down journey. When you read Dustin's poems notice the dates. Sometimes he is up and sometimes he is down. No matter where you are, that is exactly the way life is, even with God. But we are quick to know God is always with us and we know we must have faith. When the trials weigh us down God says, "My burden is light." Matthew 11:30 (NKJV) So, we pull ourselves up by our bootstraps and move forward, always remembering He is in charge and we get back to being a life-changing person with our actions and attitude.

The scripture used in this chapter has been one of my favorites, Matthew 6:33. Put God first in everything! Your life, your thoughts, make them His desires, to take his character, serve, and obey Him. In other words, do not sit idle and dwell on things in your past. This will never do you any good. Ask yourself every day what is most important in your life. People, objects, goals, and desires will compete for priority. You get to choose; choose well. Putting God first place in your life will always make you a winner.

Certainly writing down your thoughts will make you very aware of where you are headed, and it also will remind you of where you should be and how you should act. Making God priority will cause your life to line up with His Word.

The Ups and Downs

Walking and talking with Jesus first thing every morning will give you a good perspective on that day's agenda. Now, I know Satan will do his best to throw kinks in there and that is when you start praising God and if you cannot manage that, just mentioning of the name Jesus will cause demons to flee. Speak the word over your situation. There is power in the name of Jesus. Put on the full armor of God!

Dustin still has three years to keep the pace, but he has learned a great deal while incarcerated and he knows who holds tomorrow. God will never leave you or forsake you! Dustin's work has paid off, everything he has accomplished in prison has given him one year off his sentence, it has taken a lot, but the reward is great.

Keep the Pace!
Keep a good Attitude!
God First!
Can you say Hallelujah!
All praise to our God!

> "If God be for you who can stand against you?" Romans 8:31 (KJV)

> "Many are the plans in the mind of man, but it is the purpose of the Lord that will stand." Proverbs 19:21 (ESV)

> "The heart of man plans his way, But the Lord establishes his steps." Proverbs 16:9 (NKJV)

"God is faithful, who has called you into fellowship with his Son, Jesus Christ our Lord." I Corinthians 1:9 (NIV)

God has a purpose and a plan for your life. He knew you before you were formed in your mother's womb.

The Lord of hosts has sworn "As I have planned, so it will be and as I have purposed so it will happen." Isaiah 14:24 (NIV)

POEMS
BY DUSTIN C. CLOVER

MY MISTAKE
REPENTIVE HEART
SILAS AND PAUL
SEAL THE DEAL
RICH EVEN WHEN YOU'RE POOR
ENDURES FOREVER
THANK YOU, HEAVENLY FATHER,
ANY OTHER WAY
PEACE BE STILL
HIS LOVE
WHAT YOU COULD CHANGE
DON'T HOLD BACK
LIFES DECEIT
FAKE PEOPLE
SINCERITY I SPEAK
NO SHADES ON, TELL THEM THE TRUTH

MY MISTAKE

There was once a little boy who lived in the hood,
started packing pistols, hustling, doing everything he could.
Liven the G code at such a young age,
standing with his guys on the corner waiting to get paged.
Girls coming by shouting his name,
cause him and his boys was on top of their game.
This little boy was living he thought, couldn't get any better,
girls, fresh clothes, his guys and plenty of chatter.
Man this little boy had really made a name,
but the life he was living was really a shame!
Things with this life aren't always good,
this boy got a call to go to the hood.
He went to the hood to pop off a ball,
of some of that good cooked up raw.
Now at the age of 18,
dude up a gun so he had to shoot the feen.
He got out on bond and 9 months later caught another case,
man now he's really in trouble and got a lot to face.
They come with a plea as low as 10,
but he didn't take it and got 48 in the pen.
This young little boy is now 24,
he is more free then ever before.
Even though he will always be a "G",
he's changed his ways and let's God help him see.
He try's his best to reach out to the youth,
to lead them down the right path and tell them the truth.
Tell them to stay in school and do their best,
put God first in their life and he will do the rest.
So please learn from his mistakes,

Poems by Dustin C. Clover

make a life for themselves and do all it takes.
In a split decision your life can get took,
on judgment day you want your name to be in that book.
So, think ahead of time of the life you're going to take
I got 48 years for my mistake.

By Dustin Clover

REPENTIVE HEART

Dear God, I pray to you every night,
I'm really strugglin and puttin up a fight.
I wonder sometime why I still hold on,
then I thank you for keepin me strong.
I know I've done wrong things in my life,
but now I'm ready to do what's right
I want to follow under your wing,
instead of dangling under that string.
That string is what got me put in jail,
now I'm sittin here and can't even get out on bail.
I know you can do miracles and what you're about,
that's a fact I have no doubt.
I'm not giving up even though it's getting real hard
And I feel my life is falling apart.
I stay in your word and try so hard, I'm not letting the devil take my heart.
He has done enough to ruin my life,
and constantly made me have strife.
Please give me another chance and let me out,
so I can tell the world what you're about.
I'll tell them all the wonderful things you can do,
so the devil can't pick and choose.
I'm not going to let him get another life,
he's done enough wrecking and playing with mine.
Not another one is he going to play with if I lead them to Christ,
because Jesus knows what is right
And he's the one with such great might.
Soon Jesus will pick us up

Poems by Dustin C. Clover

The devil's way is real rough
So, change your life while you can,
and know Christ Jesus is the man

By Dustin Clover

SILAS AND PAUL

See I was that boy that stood my ground,
see I was that boy that wouldn't back down.
See I was that boy that didn't care,
see I was that boy my feelings I wouldn't share.
See I was that boy, pride meant all,
I was that boy that would be there in a split call.
See I was that boy that wanted respect,
I was that boy others reflect.
See I was that boy that would of taken a bullet for my homies,
the ones that when I got locked up just disowned me.
See I was that boy that being loyal was where it's at,
guess all my homies didn't think like that.
See I was that boy who almost took a guys life and left his son with out a dad
See I was that boy, that's really sad.
See I was that boy, that boy was me,
and part of that boy will forever be.
See I'm a man now and that man learned from his mistakes,
to do what's right, whatever it takes.
See that man will still slip at times, he's only human but has put away that life of crimes.
See that man now lives for the Lord,
he will still fight battles but this time it's spiritual with the sword.
That man now wants to reach out to all,
tell them about true life call.
See that man in his life was being built from gravel to solid rock,

Poems by Dustin C. Clover

when God overturns his 48 years and he comes home
people will be in shock.
See that man don't have to explain nothing at all,
but I will tell you one thing about that man, he's becoming
like Silas and Paul

By Dustin Clover

SEAL THE DEAL

I woke up one morning with a thought on my mind, so I picked up the Bible, which wasn't hard to find.

I spoke to God like you would a friend, I asked him to come into my heart and to help it unbend.

I heard a small still voce speak to my heart, "Son from the moment you were born we've never been apart!"

You've always strayed away but I've been right there; I want you to know my son I always care.

When you lost your brother you turned to the street, what kept you from dying was I covering you from your head to your feet.

Did you just think that you had good luck, but then when you caught your case your luck just suck?

No my son before you were born I knew what would take place, I knew to get you to truly live your life for me, 48 years is what you had to face.

Now that you gave me your life, left the drugs, streets and gangs behind, when you go back to court, less time is what you will find.

But from here on out you lead others to me, teach them my word and help them to see.

I tell you my son the time is near, if the people don't give their lives to me hell they should fear.

I answered with a loud voice, thank you Heavenly Father for this choice.

No one wants to burn in hell, so your word I will speak and tell.

Thank you, Heavenly Father, for forgiving me of my sin, and giving me this talent to write poetry with this pen.

I tell all of you, now is the time to kneel and pray, no matter what you have done He will forgive you and make you a new person today.

Nobody knows what tomorrow might bring, give your life to God and cut them sins away that's dangling from that string.

I tell you heaven and hell are real, so before it's too late Seal the Deal!!!

By Dustin Clover 2/5/2011

Look at Me Now

RICH EVEN WHEN YOU'RE POOR

Im'a real G and there's no way to change it,
here's the money for my casket go ahead and arrange it.
In the hood slinging everything you can think,
get out you body and I'll dump that pistol before you can blink.
Stay on my grind and fresher than ever,
I got a personality that will put a smile on your face even when you're under the weather.
At eighteen I caught an attempt when no one was around,
fam upped the pistol so I put him to the ground.
I'm not saying any of this proudly only trying to make a point,
the streets will have you end up like me with forty-eight years in the joint.
Listen to me I've changed my life will you please do the same,
there is so much more to life than playing that deadly game.
I gave my life to God he turned it completely around,
for the guys, still got love, but no longer gettin down.
I'm truly free than ever before,
I got my case back in court and I know God will soon open up this prison door.
I pray you give your life to God before it's too late,
God built us a mansion; it's up to us if we make it on the other side of that gate.
Be aware, you can't steal, cheat, lie or shoot you way through that heavenly door,
you can be so much happier not being rich on earth
But with God you're rich even when you're poor.

By Dustin Clover 9/2011

Poems by Dustin C. Clover

ENDURES FOREVER

I have that pretty boy swag,
stay fresh, gangstad and neva thought about dropping my flag
I would have done anything for the team,
so young, done more than most have seen.
If it had to do something with the streets,
I've done almost all you can think of on this earth,
momma didn't know her son was going to be a gangsta at birth.
I had it all, girls, fresh clothes, and plenty of chetta,
I thought to myself this life couldn't get any better.
In all reality my soul was lost,
caught up in the streets, forty-eight years is what it cost.
At one point I let the devil steal my dreams,
I truly gave my life to the Lord,
then he showed me things are going to be much easier than it seems.
Stay in his word and he will provide all,
if you do he won't let you fall.
I'm twenty-five been a gangsta since I was ten,
Take my word that life gets you no where,
it got me sitting with forty-eight years in the state pen.
I'm no longer reepin for my crew in the hood,
only reepin for Christ lets make that understood.
The guys aren't here,
the hood don't care.
Go ahead and give it up to God his love he wants to share.
God's love endures forever
When you're gone the streets love is never.

By Dustin Clover October 10, 2011

THANK YOU HEAVENLY FATHER

Today is a day to give you all the thanks, honor and glory, so, Heavenly Father let me first say, thanks for my life story.
I thank you in the morning, I thank you in the day.
I thank you Heavenly Father for blessing me in every way.
You've blessed me with such a wonderful mother.
Heavenly Father for sending your son to pay the price for our sin.
I thank you for all that you've done and for you, lives, I will try to win.
I thank you Heavenly Father for changing my life from the street.
To picking up your word and binding Satan with defeat.
Heavenly Father your love is so real.
Some say it's just the imagination but for me it's something I truly feel.
Heavenly Father you're so awesome and I love you so much.
Some say you're just a spirit but to me you're someone I can touch.
Thank you, Heavenly Father, for being someone I can lean on and trust
Picking up your word daily to me that's a must.

By Dustin Clover 11/6/2011

ANY OTHER WAY

Father God, I ask that you will stand by me as I walk through the day,
help me through this dark world and with the things I want to say.
Father God, the devil is lurking twenty four seven,
but I want you to know I'm doing all I can to stand firm and help others get to heaven.
I know I've fallen in times of despair,
but I know when others don't, you always care.
I thank you Father for helping me back to my feet,
time and time again the devil thought he had another one with defeat.
I refuse not to stand my ground,
I loose warring angels, devil you are bound.
Satan I command you to flee, my past is my past, with Christ I must be.
You will not get me to go back to my old ways.
Living as a gangster in those cold dark days.
Flesh of my flesh, blood of my blood,
but through Christ the old me is now a dud
Christ didn't just pay the price for me, but for you as well,
open up His word and begin to read, He has so much to tell.
If you will speak His word and accept Him in your life,
I'm not saying it will be easy, but you will have much less strife.
So open up His word and begin to read today.

I promise you, you will feel His presence and won't ever want it any other way.

By Dustin Clover 2013

PEACE BE STILL

Father God I ask that you will speak to me, help me to do your will.
Give me vision on what you want done...son peace be still.
Son I know you've gone through a lot, but I'm using that for my glory.
This will be a testimony you will use, your life story.
I'm releasing you soon and you will share with all,
the thing's I've done for you when you reached out and called.
Stay true to my word, I will give you all you need,
and that son you want, in my time you will succeed.
You see my son, I'm planning your life, I have you in the palm of my hand.
I need you to ground your roots and continue to take a stand.
I place people in your life for many reasons,
some for just a month, some a lifetime, others just a season.
There are reasons I do this. It's important for you to plant God's seed
So others can continue to plant and off God's word feed.
My son you always get in a hurry, that is why I said peace be still,
Let me work my plan and your dreams will be fulfilled.

By Dustin Clover 10/6/2013

HIS LOVE

I was headed for death, on my last breath,
out of control, til God saved my soul.
I gave it to him, my life's no longer dim.
I see the light, it suddenly got bright.
Sentenced to 48 years in prison, because of poor decisions.
God opened up the door,
when I landed on my knees and bowed on the floor.
I walk with him daily, He's my best friend,
when no one else cares, His love He always sends

By Dustin Clover 12/23/2013

WHAT YOU COULD CHANGE

I grew up a gansta and my heart is still real,
but my old ways is no longer how I feel.
I've put my mother and family through so much because
of my past, and the time you try to get back, just goes
by so fast.
Constantly in pain, so mad and down,
no smile at all, only a frown.
Feel that the world has given up hope,
all I use to do was pop pistols and sell dope.
I realize now that's nothing but destruction,
and if you don't watch out, the world is full of corruption.
They'll pull you down and get you in a hold,
they'll talk slick but their heart's really cold.
I've learned from my mistakes and I look to the light,
pick up my bible daily and keep the cross in my sight.
If you'll do the same the world could be rearranged,
all through faith and prayer, if you only knew what you
could change.

By Dustin Clover 1/29/2014

DON'T HOLD BACK

I use to walk the life of death,
God could have taken my last breath...but didn't
I'm alive and well, no matter if I am in a prison cell.
On the streets I stayed super high,
posted up making money and if needed letting bullets fly.
Sometimes I wonder the reason why?
Then I found God or actually he found me,
started changing my ways and seeing who I'm really suppose to be.
A disciple for Christ, bring others to Him.
Allowing them to see, their lives don't have to be dim.
See everyone has a divine purpose and plan, it's ultimately up to you
Whether you take that and put it in God's hand.
There are so many lives that need to be touched,
I'm here to tell you God loves you so much.
No matter what you have done, or where you've gone wrong
Christ took that to the cross, and He will keep you strong.
See I was a sinner and so lost, I almost took a guy's life and so much it has cost.
I'm no longer lost, I'm no longer bound,
through Christ Jesus I have been found.
You can be found just like me, If you will ask Christ to come into your heart and allow him to see.
Don't hold back, your next breath might be too late,
the devil is lurking for his next date.

By Dustin Clover 4/13/14

LIFE'S DECEIT

I'm still pleading for another chance at life,
several years now and they're still stabbing my plea with a knife.
The system is so unjust,
but if someone makes them a plea, life sentence is a must.
It's crazy how the things in the system turn,
you make a split mistake and It's your life to burn.
But if they do something it's swept under the rug,
crazy how they can shoot someone with a slug.
I guess this is just the life of the court,
pick which side and the type of sport.
Life with a badge or the life of the street
Whichever life it's full of deceit,
a life that's happy, full and complete.
They say will only be in heaven when God we meet.

By Dustin Clover 10/1/2015

FAKE PEOPLE

As my days turn to sorrow and my nights continue to pass,
I sit here and ponder about those in my past.
I wonder where I went wrong in my life beyond the wall,
I stayed true and real but none came to my call.
For all who folded under the drop of a hat,
it's crazy how everyone continues like nothing happened like that.
But doing this time has helped me see the real truth,
Of all I believed in since my youth.
So many of you are fake, you can't even come forward to make things right,
I hope it weighs on your mind and you can't sleep at night.
You have an innocent man losing his life by the day,
now for that of course you have nothing to say.
I can say this, I admit I've done my fare share, my time I've already spared.
I don't want sympathy or sorrow,
I just want you to come forward and tell the truth so my family can see a better tomorrow.
I'd really like to know if tomorrow I was placed in my casket and buried away,
how many would come to my funeral and have something to say.
Would people be too busy, just come for the show, or would you be for real,
how many would continue to come after the whole ordeal
I'd imagine it would still be like my past 10 years
My mother visiting once a week still shedding tears

My father, aunt, cousin, and niece coming when they are able,
if this was to happen in your life how could you remain stable?
Please don't feel sorry I'm doing just fine
I just want you to think about other's lives that are on the line.
For all who think they know about the system in anyway,
I suggest you truly do research before you have anything to say.

By Dustin Clover 9/7/2015

SINCERITY I SPEAK

This is still no grant to my plea
So many lies, I let it be.
True to my word I hold it down
So many fake, nowhere around.
They said they were going to release me, now my grandma passed,
I know she's in a better place, but my mind is racing fast.
So many questions do I ask
All politics hiding behind a mask.
Few to none are truly real,
most are imposters, just sayin how I feel.
Trust none, expect all
Cause your right hand man will give you up when ya'll fall
Sometimes we question if God really hears
If he's real, I know he sees these tears
But I'm a soldier I'm as real as they get,
Wipe these tears and keep doing this bit.
My mom, girl and family still holding me down
Ima give it to God see if He turns it around.
I've done everything under the earth
Momma did her best ever since my birth.
But she's proud I've changed my ways.
I allow God to control my days.
So from here on out God it's you I seek,
Hear my prayer and the sincerity I speak.

By Dustin Clover 5/28/2017

Poems by Dustin C. Clover

NO SHADES ON, TELL THEM THE TRUTH

For all of you that think you know me because maybe someone you know did a bit,
watch what you say because you don't know shit.
You wouldn't stand a chance if you had to do what I've did,
I took the weight and didn't say nothing, while you would've run and hid
But yeah you talkin shit and you don't even know me,
Talking bout let's hope he's not the same when comes home you really starting to blow me.
The old me would hit that slide,
pull out that drum and let it ride.
Choppa on hand homie until I die.
But see that's the life that got me with a total of 61 years, so
For the ones that think I'm the same, please just stay clear.
I'm as real as they come and stay true to my word,
I don't want to be looked at like the old me because I look to God's word.
All of you speculate like everyone's the same, oh, he went to prison he's still in the game.
Yeah I still struggle, yeah I've slipped,
but I stayed real while most you all flipped.
I progress daily to get home to have a life,
to be with the love of my life who one day I may call wife.
I lived the streets and it only leads to destruction,
If they want you bad enough even if you didn't do it there's corruption.
I admit I've done plenty in my past,
if you haven't, take the stone and cast.
But the time I'm serving now is corruption at hand,

Look at Me Now

If you have a heart at all please take a stand.
I only want to come home, live a productive life and reach out to the youth,
tell them what the streets got me no shades on, tell them the truth!

By Dustin Clover 10/13/19

THIS IS NOT THE END OF DUSTIN CALEB CLOVER'S STORY,

HE WANTS YOU ALL TO KNOW HIS LIFE IS IN GOD'S HANDS!

IT ALWAYS WAS AND HE GIVES GOD THE GLORY.

Walking this road with my Nephew, he and I felt a need to show all there is hope for those who are willing to trust God.

www.ingramcontent.com/pod-product-compliance
Ingram Content Group UK Ltd.
Pitfield, Milton Keynes, MK11 3LW, UK
UKHW041949230426
12048UKWH00008B/233